Tattoo

Placement

Theme

Planned Date

Palette

Placement

Design

Detail 1

Detail 2

Notes

Tattoo

Placement

Theme

Planned Date

Palette

Placement

Design

Detail 1

Detail 2

Notes

Tattoo

Placement

Theme

Planned Date

Palette

Placement

Design

Detail 1

Detail 2

Notes

Tattoo

Placement

Theme

Planned Date

Palette

Placement

Design

Detail 1

Detail 2

Notes

Tattoo

Placement

Theme

Planned Date

Palette

Placement

Design

Detail 1

Detail 2

Notes

Tattoo

Placement

Theme

Planned Date

Palette

Placement

Design

Detail 1

Detail 2

Notes

Tattoo

Placement

Theme

Planned Date

Palette

Placement

Design

Detail 1

Detail 2

Notes

Tattoo

Placement

Theme

Planned Date

Palette

Placement

Design

Detail 1

Detail 2

Notes

Tattoo

Placement

Theme

Planned Date

Palette

Placement

Design

Detail 1

Detail 2

Notes

Tattoo

Placement

Theme

Planned Date

Placement

Palette

Design

Detail 1

Detail 2

Notes

Tattoo

Placement

Theme

Planned Date

Palette

Placement

Design

Detail 1

Detail 2

Notes

Tattoo

Placement

Theme

Planned Date

Palette

Placement

Design

Detail 1

Detail 2

Notes

Tattoo

Placement

Theme

Planned Date

Palette

Placement

Design

Detail 1

Detail 2

Notes

Tattoo

Placement

Theme

Planned Date

Palette

Placement

Design

Detail 1

Detail 2

Notes

Tattoo

Placement

Theme

Planned Date

Palette

Placement

Design

Detail 1

Detail 2

Notes

Tattoo

Placement

Theme

Planned Date

Palette

Placement

Design

Detail 1

Detail 2

Notes

Tattoo

Placement

Theme

Planned Date

Palette

Placement

Design

Detail 1

Detail 2

Notes

Tattoo

Placement

Theme

Planned Date

Palette

Placement

Design

Detail 1

Detail 2

Notes

Tattoo

Placement

Theme

Planned Date

Palette

Placement

Design

Detail 1

Detail 2

Notes

Tattoo

Placement

Theme

Planned Date

Palette

Placement

Design

Detail 1

Detail 2

Notes

Tattoo

Placement

Theme

Planned Date

Palette

Placement

Design

Detail 1

Detail 2

Notes

Tattoo

Placement

Theme

Planned Date

Placement

Palette

Design

Detail 1

Detail 2

Notes

Tattoo

Placement

Theme

Planned Date

Placement

Palette

Design

Detail 1

Detail 2

Notes

Tattoo

Placement

Theme

Planned Date

Palette

Placement

Design

Detail 1

Detail 2

Notes

Tattoo

Placement

Theme

Planned Date

Palette

Placement

Design

Detail 1

Detail 2

Notes

Tattoo

Placement

Theme

Planned Date

Palette

Placement

Design

Detail 1

Detail 2

Notes

Tattoo

Placement

Theme

Planned Date

Palette

Placement

Design

Detail 1

Detail 2

Notes

Tattoo

Placement

Theme

Planned Date

Palette

Placement

Design

Detail 1

Detail 2

Notes

Tattoo

Placement

Theme

Planned Date

Palette

Placement

Design

Detail 1

Detail 2

Notes

Tattoo

Placement

Theme

Planned Date

Palette

Placement

Design

Detail 1

Detail 2

Notes

Tattoo

Placement

Theme

Planned Date

Palette

Placement

Design

Detail 1

Detail 2

Notes

Tattoo

Placement

Theme

Planned Date

Placement

Palette

Design

Detail 1

Detail 2

Notes

Tattoo

Placement

Theme

Planned Date

Palette

Placement

Design

Detail 1

Detail 2

Notes

Tattoo

Placement

Theme

Planned Date

Palette

Placement

Design

Detail 1

Detail 2

Notes

Tattoo

Placement

Theme

Planned Date

Palette

Placement

Design

Detail 1

Detail 2

Notes

Tattoo

Placement

Theme

Planned Date

Placement

Palette

Design

Detail 1

Detail 2

Notes

Tattoo

Placement

Theme

Planned Date

Placement

Palette

Design

Detail 1

Detail 2

Notes

Tattoo

Placement

Theme

Planned Date

Palette

Placement

Design

Detail 1

Detail 2

Notes

Tattoo

Placement

Theme

Planned Date

Palette

Placement

Design

Detail 1

Detail 2

Notes

Tattoo

Placement

Theme

Planned Date

Palette

Placement

Design

Detail 1

Detail 2

Notes

Tattoo

Placement

Theme

Planned Date

Palette

Placement

Design

Detail 1

Detail 2

Notes

Tattoo

Placement

Theme

Planned Date

Palette

Placement

Design

Detail 1

Detail 2

Notes

Tattoo

Placement

Theme

Planned Date

Palette

Placement

Design

Detail 1

Detail 2

Notes

Tattoo

Placement

Theme

Planned Date

Palette

Placement

Design

Detail 1

Detail 2

Notes

Tattoo

Placement

Theme

Planned Date

Palette

Placement

Design

Detail 1

Detail 2

Notes

Tattoo

Placement

Theme

Planned Date

Palette

Placement

Design

Detail 1

Detail 2

Notes

Tattoo

Placement

Theme

Planned Date

Placement

Palette

Design

Detail 1

Detail 2

Notes

Tattoo

Placement

Theme

Planned Date

Palette

Placement

Design

Detail 1

Detail 2

Notes

Tattoo

Placement

Theme

Planned Date

Palette

Placement

Design

Detail 1

Detail 2

Notes

Tattoo

Placement

Theme

Planned Date

Palette

Placement

Design

Detail 1

Detail 2

Notes

Tattoo

Placement

Theme

Planned Date

Palette

Placement

Design

Detail 1

Detail 2

Notes

Tattoo

Placement

Theme

Planned Date

Palette

Placement

Design

Detail 1

Detail 2

Notes

Tattoo

Placement

Theme

Planned Date

Palette

Placement

Design

Detail 1

Detail 2

Notes

Tattoo

Placement

Theme

Planned Date

Palette

Placement

Design

Detail 1

Detail 2

Notes

Tattoo

Placement

Theme

Planned Date

Palette

Placement

Design

Detail 1

Detail 2

Notes

Tattoo

Placement

Theme

Planned Date

Palette

Placement

Design

Detail 1

Detail 2

Notes

Tattoo

Placement

Theme

Planned Date

Palette

Placement

Design

Detail 1

Detail 2

Notes

Tattoo

Placement

Theme

Planned Date

Palette

Placement

Design

Detail 1

Detail 2

Notes

Tattoo

Placement

Theme

Planned Date

Palette

Placement

Design

Detail 1

Detail 2

Notes

Tattoo

Placement

Theme

Planned Date

Palette

Placement

Design

Detail 1

Detail 2

Notes

Tattoo

Placement

Theme

Planned Date

Palette

Placement

Design

Detail 1

Detail 2

Notes

Tattoo

Placement

Theme

Planned Date

Palette

Placement

Design

Detail 1

Detail 2

Notes

Tattoo

Placement

Theme

Planned Date

Palette

Placement

Design

Detail 1

Detail 2

Notes

Tattoo

Placement

Theme

Planned Date

Palette

Placement

Design

Detail 1

Detail 2

Notes

Tattoo

Placement

Theme

Planned Date

Palette

Placement

Design

Detail 1

Detail 2

Notes

Tattoo

Placement

Theme

Planned Date

Palette

Placement

Design

Detail 1

Detail 2

Notes

Tattoo

Placement

Theme

Planned Date

Palette

Placement

Design

Detail 1

Detail 2

Notes

Tattoo

Placement

Theme

Planned Date

Palette

Placement

Design

Detail 1

Detail 2

Notes

Tattoo

Placement

Theme

Planned Date

Palette

Design

Placement

Detail 1

Detail 2

Notes

Tattoo

Placement

Theme

Planned Date

Palette

Placement

Design

Detail 1

Detail 2

Notes

Tattoo

Placement

Theme

Planned Date

Palette

Placement

Design

Detail 1

Detail 2

Notes

Tattoo

Placement

Theme

Planned Date

Placement

Palette

Design

Detail 1

Detail 2

Notes

Tattoo

Placement

Theme

Planned Date

Palette

Placement

Design

Detail 1

Detail 2

Notes

Tattoo

Placement

Theme

Planned Date

Placement

Palette

Design

Detail 1

Detail 2

Notes

Tattoo

Placement

Theme

Planned Date

Palette

Placement

Design

Detail 1

Detail 2

Notes

Tattoo

Placement

Theme

Planned Date

Placement

Palette

Design

Detail 1

Detail 2

Notes

Tattoo

Placement

Theme

Planned Date

Palette

Design

Placement

Detail 1

Detail 2

Notes

Tattoo

Placement

Theme

Planned Date

Palette

Placement

Design

Detail 1

Detail 2

Notes

Tattoo

Placement

Theme

Planned Date

Palette

Placement

Design

Detail 1

Detail 2

Notes

Tattoo

Placement

Theme

Planned Date

Palette

Placement

Design

Detail 1

Detail 2

Notes

Tattoo

Placement

Theme

Planned Date

Palette

Placement

Design

Detail 1

Detail 2

Notes

Tattoo

Placement

Theme

Planned Date

Palette

Placement

Design

Detail 1

Detail 2

Notes

Tattoo

Placement

Theme

Planned Date

Placement

Palette

Design

Detail 1

Detail 2

Notes

Tattoo

Placement

Theme

Planned Date

Palette

Placement

Design

Detail 1

Detail 2

Notes

Tattoo

Placement

Theme

Planned Date

Palette

Placement

Design

Detail 1

Detail 2

Notes

Tattoo

Placement

Theme

Planned Date

Palette

Placement

Design

Detail 1

Detail 2

Notes

Tattoo

Placement

Theme

Planned Date

Palette

Placement

Design

Detail 1

Detail 2

Notes

Tattoo

Placement

Theme

Planned Date

Palette

Placement

Design

Detail 1

Detail 2

Notes

Tattoo

Placement

Theme

Planned Date

Palette

Placement

Design

Detail 1

Detail 2

Notes

Tattoo

Placement

Theme

Planned Date

Palette

Placement

Design

Detail 1

Detail 2

Notes

Tattoo

Placement

Theme

Planned Date

Palette

Placement

Design

Detail 1

Detail 2

Notes

Tattoo

Placement

Theme

Planned Date

Palette

Placement

Design

Detail 1

Detail 2

Notes

Tattoo

Placement

Theme

Planned Date

Palette

Placement

Design

Detail 1

Detail 2

Notes

Tattoo

Placement

Theme

Planned Date

Placement

Palette

Design

Detail 1

Detail 2

Notes

Tattoo

Placement

Theme

Planned Date

Palette

Placement

Design

Detail 1

Detail 2

Notes

Tattoo

Placement

Theme

Planned Date

Palette

Placement

Design

Detail 1

Detail 2

Notes

Tattoo

Placement

Theme

Planned Date

Palette

Placement

Design

Detail 1

Detail 2

Notes

Tattoo

Placement

Theme

Planned Date

Palette

Placement

Design

Detail 1

Detail 2

Notes

Tattoo

Placement

Theme

Planned Date

Placement

Palette

Design

Detail 1

Detail 2

Notes

Tattoo

Placement

Theme

Planned Date

Placement

Palette

Design

Detail 1

Detail 2

Notes

Tattoo

Placement

Theme

Planned Date

Palette

Placement

Design

Detail 1

Detail 2

Notes

Tattoo

Placement

Theme

Planned Date

Palette

Placement

Design

Detail 1

Detail 2

Notes

Tattoo

Placement

Theme

Planned Date

Placement

Palette

Design

Detail 1

Detail 2

Notes

Tattoo

Placement

Theme

Planned Date

Palette

Placement

Design

Detail 1

Detail 2

Notes

Tattoo

Placement

Theme

Planned Date

Palette

Placement

Design

Detail 1

Detail 2

Notes

Tattoo

Placement

Theme

Planned Date

Palette

Placement

Design

Detail 1

Detail 2

Notes

Tattoo

Placement

Theme

Planned Date

Placement

Palette

Design

Detail 1

Detail 2

Notes

Tattoo

Placement

Theme

Planned Date

Palette

Placement

Design

Detail 1

Detail 2

Notes

Tattoo

Placement

Theme

Planned Date

Palette

Placement

Design

Detail 1

Detail 2

Notes

Tattoo

Placement

Theme

Planned Date

Placement

Palette

Design

Detail 1

Detail 2

Notes

Tattoo

Placement

Theme

Planned Date

Palette

Design

Placement

Detail 1

Detail 2

Notes

Tattoo

Placement

Theme

Planned Date

Placement

Palette

Design

Detail 1

Detail 2

Notes

Tattoo

Placement

Theme

Planned Date

Palette

Design

Placement

Detail 1

Detail 2

Notes

Tattoo

Placement

Theme

Planned Date

Palette

Placement

Design

Detail 1

Detail 2

Notes

Tattoo

Placement

Theme

Planned Date

Palette

Placement

Design

Detail 1

Detail 2

Notes

Tattoo

Placement

Theme

Planned Date

Palette

Placement

Design

Detail 1

Detail 2

Notes

Tattoo

Placement

Theme

Planned Date

Palette

Placement

Design

Detail 1

Detail 2

Notes

Tattoo

Placement

Theme

Planned Date

Placement

Palette

Design

Detail 1

Detail 2

Notes

Tattoo

Placement

Theme

Planned Date

Palette

Placement

Design

Detail 1

Detail 2

Notes

Tattoo

Placement

Theme

Planned Date

Palette

Placement

Design

Detail 1

Detail 2

Notes

Tattoo

Placement

Theme

Planned Date

Palette

Placement

Design

Detail 1

Detail 2

Notes

Tattoo

Placement

Theme

Planned Date

Palette

Placement

Design

Detail 1

Detail 2

Notes

Tattoo

Placement

Theme

Planned Date

Palette

Placement

Design

Detail 1

Detail 2

Notes

Tattoo

Placement

Theme

Planned Date

Palette

Placement

Design

Detail 1

Detail 2

Notes

Tattoo

Placement

Theme

Planned Date

Palette

Placement

Design

Detail 1

Detail 2

Notes

Tattoo

Placement

Theme

Planned Date

Palette

Placement

Design

Detail 1

Detail 2

Notes

Tattoo

Placement

Theme

Planned Date

Palette

Placement

Design

Detail 1

Detail 2

Notes

Tattoo

Placement

Theme

Planned Date

Palette

Placement

Design

Detail 1

Detail 2

Notes

Tattoo

Placement

Theme

Planned Date

Palette

Design

Placement

Detail 1

Detail 2

Notes

Tattoo

Placement

Theme

Planned Date

Palette

Placement

Design

Detail 1

Detail 2

Notes

Tattoo

Placement

Theme

Planned Date

Placement

Palette

Design

Detail 1

Detail 2

Notes

Tattoo

Placement

Theme

Planned Date

Palette

Placement

Design

Detail 1

Detail 2

Notes

Tattoo

Placement

Theme

Planned Date

Palette

Placement

Design

Detail 1

Detail 2

Notes

Tattoo

Placement

Theme

Planned Date

Palette

Placement

Design

Detail 1

Detail 2

Notes

Tattoo

Placement

Theme

Planned Date

Palette

Placement

Design

Detail 1

Detail 2

Notes

Tattoo

Placement

Theme

Planned Date

Palette

Placement

Design

Detail 1

Detail 2

Notes

Tattoo

Placement

Theme

Planned Date

Palette

Placement

Design

Detail 1

Detail 2

Notes

Tattoo

Placement

Theme

Planned Date

Palette

Placement

Design

Detail 1

Detail 2

Notes

Tattoo

Placement

Theme

Planned Date

Palette

Placement

Design

Detail 1

Detail 2

Notes

Tattoo

Placement

Theme

Planned Date

Palette

Placement

Design

Detail 1

Detail 2

Notes

Tattoo

Placement

Theme

Planned Date

Palette

Placement

Design

Detail 1

Detail 2

Notes

Tattoo

Placement

Theme

Planned Date

Palette

Placement

Design

Detail 1

Detail 2

Notes

Tattoo

Placement

Theme

Planned Date

Palette

Placement

Design

Detail 1

Detail 2

Notes

Tattoo

Placement

Theme

Planned Date

Palette

Placement

Design

Detail 1

Detail 2

Notes

Tattoo

Placement

Theme

Planned Date

Placement

Palette

Design

Detail 1

Detail 2

Notes

Tattoo

Placement

Theme

Planned Date

Palette

Placement

Design

Detail 1

Detail 2

Notes

Tattoo

Placement

Theme

Planned Date

Palette

Placement

Design

Detail 1

Detail 2

Notes

Tattoo

Placement

Theme

Planned Date

Palette

Placement

Design

Detail 1

Detail 2

Notes

Tattoo

Placement

Theme

Planned Date

Placement

Palette

Design

Detail 1

Detail 2

Notes

Tattoo

Placement

Theme

Planned Date

Palette

Placement

Design

Detail 1

Detail 2

Notes

Tattoo

Placement

Theme

Planned Date

Placement

Palette

Design

Detail 1

Detail 2

Notes

Tattoo

Placement

Theme

Planned Date

Palette

Placement

Design

Detail 1

Detail 2

Notes

Tattoo

Placement

Theme

Planned Date

Palette

Placement

Design

Detail 1

Detail 2

Notes

Tattoo

Placement

Theme

Planned Date

Palette

Placement

Design

Detail 1

Detail 2

Notes

Tattoo

Placement

Theme

Planned Date

Placement

Palette

Design

Detail 1

Detail 2

Notes

Tattoo

Placement

Theme

Planned Date

Palette

Placement

Design

Detail 1

Detail 2

Notes

Tattoo

Placement

Theme

Planned Date

Palette

Placement

Design

Detail 1

Detail 2

Notes

Tattoo

Placement

Theme

Planned Date

Palette

Placement

Design

Detail 1

Detail 2

Notes

Tattoo

Placement

Theme

Planned Date

Placement

Palette

Design

Detail 1

Detail 2

Notes

Tattoo

Placement

Theme

Planned Date

Placement

Palette

Design

Detail 1

Detail 2

Notes

Tattoo

Placement

Theme

Planned Date

Palette

Placement

Design

Detail 1

Detail 2

Notes

Tattoo

Placement

Theme

Planned Date

Palette

Placement

Design

Detail 1

Detail 2

Notes

Tattoo

Placement

Theme

Planned Date

Palette

Placement

Design

Detail 1

Detail 2

Notes

Tattoo

Placement

Theme

Planned Date

Palette

Placement

Design

Detail 1

Detail 2

Notes

Tattoo

Placement

Theme

Planned Date

Palette

Placement

Design

Detail 1

Detail 2

Notes

Tattoo

Placement

Theme

Planned Date

Palette

Placement

Design

Detail 1

Detail 2

Notes

Tattoo

Placement

Theme

Planned Date

Placement

Palette

Design

Detail 1

Detail 2

Notes

Tattoo

Placement

Theme

Planned Date

Placement

Palette

Design

Detail 1

Detail 2

Notes

Tattoo

Placement

Theme

Planned Date

Placement

Palette

Design

Detail 1

Detail 2

Notes

Tattoo

Placement

Theme

Planned Date

Palette

Placement

Design

Detail 1

Detail 2

Notes

Tattoo

Placement

Theme

Planned Date

Placement

Palette

Design

Detail 1

Detail 2

Notes

Tattoo

Placement

Theme

Planned Date

Palette

Placement

Design

Detail 1

Detail 2

Notes

Tattoo

Placement

Theme

Planned Date

Palette

Placement

Design

Detail 1

Detail 2

Notes

Tattoo

Placement

Theme

Planned Date

Palette

Placement

Design

Detail 1

Detail 2

Notes

Tattoo

Placement

Theme

Planned Date

Placement

Palette

Design

Detail 1

Detail 2

Notes

Tattoo

Placement

Theme

Planned Date

Palette

Placement

Design

Detail 1

Detail 2

Notes

Tattoo

Placement

Theme

Planned Date

Palette

Placement

Design

Detail 1

Detail 2

Notes

Tattoo

Placement

Theme

Planned Date

Palette

Placement

Design

Detail 1

Detail 2

Notes

Tattoo

Placement

Theme

Planned Date

Placement

Palette

Design

Detail 1

Detail 2

Notes

Tattoo

Placement

Theme

Planned Date

Palette

Placement

Design

Detail 1

Detail 2

Notes

Tattoo

Placement

Theme

Planned Date

Placement

Palette

Design

Detail 1

Detail 2

Notes

Tattoo

Placement

Theme

Planned Date

Palette

Placement

Design

Detail 1

Detail 2

Notes

Tattoo

Placement

Theme

Planned Date

Palette

Placement

Design

Detail 1

Detail 2

Notes

Tattoo

Placement

Theme

Planned Date

Placement

Palette

Design

Detail 1

Detail 2

Notes

Tattoo

Placement

Theme

Planned Date

Palette

Placement

Design

Detail 1

Detail 2

Notes

Tattoo

Placement

Theme

Planned Date

Palette

Placement

Design

Detail 1

Detail 2

Notes

Tattoo

Placement

Theme

Planned Date

Palette

Placement

Design

Detail 1

Detail 2

Notes

Tattoo

Placement

Theme

Planned Date

Palette

Placement

Design

Detail 1

Detail 2

Notes

Tattoo

Placement

Theme

Planned Date

Palette

Placement

Design

Detail 1

Detail 2

Notes

Tattoo

Placement

Theme

Planned Date

Palette

Placement

Design

Detail 1

Detail 2

Notes

Tattoo

Placement

Theme

Planned Date

Palette

Placement

Design

Detail 1

Detail 2

Notes

Tattoo

Placement

Theme

Planned Date

Palette

Placement

Design

Detail 1

Detail 2

Notes

Tattoo

Placement

Theme

Planned Date

Palette

Placement

Design

Detail 1

Detail 2

Notes

Tattoo

Placement

Theme

Planned Date

Palette

Placement

Design

Detail 1

Detail 2

Notes

Tattoo

Placement

Theme

Planned Date

Placement

Palette

Design

Detail 1

Detail 2

Notes

Tattoo

Placement

Theme

Planned Date

Palette

Placement

Design

Detail 1

Detail 2

Notes

Tattoo

Placement

Theme

Planned Date

Palette

Placement

Design

Detail 1

Detail 2

Notes

Tattoo

Placement

Theme

Planned Date

Palette

Placement

Design

Detail 1

Detail 2

Notes

Tattoo

Placement

Theme

Planned Date

Palette

Placement

Design

Detail 1

Detail 2

Notes

Tattoo

Placement

Theme

Planned Date

Placement

Palette

Design

Detail 1

Detail 2

Notes

www.ingramcontent.com/pod-product-compliance
Lightning Source LLC
Chambersburg PA
CBHW081428220526
45466CB00008B/2300